AUSTRALIA

THE FOUR SEASONS

A U S T R A L I A

THE FOUR SEASONS

ERIC ROLLS • REG LIVERMORE • BOB BROWN • OODGEROO NOONUCCAL

ANGUS
& ROBERTSON
PUBLISHERS

Produced by Bow Press,
208 Victoria Road,
Drummoyne, NSW, 2047 for

ANGUS & ROBERTSON PUBLISHERS

Unit 4, Eden Park, 31 Waterloo Road,
North Ryde, NSW, Australia 2113
94 Newton Road, Auckland 1,
New Zealand; and
16 Golden Square, London W1R 4BN,
United Kingdom

First published in Australia
by Angus & Robertson Publishers in 1989.
First published in New Zealand
by Angus & Robertson NZ Ltd in 1989.
First published in the United Kingdom
by Angus & Robertson (UK) in 1989.

Copyright © Bow Press
Copyright in the individual essays remains with the author

National Library of Australia
Cataloguing-in Publication data.

Australia. The four seasons.

ISBN 0 207 16191 7.

1. Seasons — Australia. 2 Seasons — Australia
— Pictorial works. I. Livermore, Reg.

525'.5'0994

Typeset in Australia by Excel Imaging Pty Ltd, Sydney
Printed in Singapore by Tien Wah Press
Production by Vantage Graphics, Sydney
Set in Modern 11/14 compressed

Designed by Bruno Grasswill
Front cover photo: Australian Tourist Commission

Three faces of the country
. . . the wheatfields
stretch to the horizon and
beyond.
PREVIOUS PAGE: The endless
outback. FOLLOWING PAGE:
Mustering sheep on the
lush banks of a quiet
stream.

CONTENTS

Introduction

IN THE HEAT of mid-summer, when the temperature tops 40ºC and it's one of those thankfully rare days when the humidity seems to be running parallel we pine for the cool mornings of autumn, even the cold noons of winter.

In the grip of winter, when four blankets have no power, when the wind is howling outside the bedroom window and the for the fifth dawn in a row the rain is pelting against the glass, we yearn for the clear skies and warmth of summer.

The clean brittle mornings of autumn, when the rust carpet of leaves crackles underfoot. Or the lush early light of spring, when wildflowers spread out in a blaze of colour.

The seasons in Australia do exist. Man thumbs his nose at nature and arbitrarily declares set dates for the start of each season: December 1 (summer), March 1 (autumn), June 1 (winter), September 1 (spring). Nature nods obligingly at the calendar and then happily does what she pleases. Summers can run on for more than a month or start late and finish early. Autumn can be a fleeting wind-blown few weeks before the onrush of an early winter. Our seasons may not occur as generally or be as clearly defined as in the Northern Hemisphere but they all have their place in this island continent. And they all have their admirers . . .

Conservationist Dr Bob Brown defends winter. He admits, albeit grudgingly, that it is not a popular season. But he describes the cold term with warmth. It takes a rare love for a season to talk of socks which had set like slices of wood, needing a fire to thaw them out — and make it seem almost a blessing. It is his season for hugging, for friends, for nature's clearing of the decks.

Author Eric Rolls sees life in spring. The fields that need the grain rain; the deserts transformed by sudden rain; the wildlife that floods the Murray River with spring. The mating and meeting. The magical, too brief flurry of growth that accompanies the new new hope each spring brings.

Actor, writer and late-blooming gardener Reg Livermore enjoys the show of autumn. The dried-out curtains of summer are pulled back and autumn takes centre-stage, not drifting in from the wings but bouncing on assertively. Autumn, with its mature, proud colours has arrived. As he admits, the theatricality of the season holds one of its greatest appeals. It is a time for lingering walks and taking stock.

Oodgeroo of the tribe Noonuccal, formerly Kath Walker, sees poetry in summer. And despair. She welcomes summer's arrival but dreads the accompaniments: the tourists in their 4WD vehicles, the casual fishermen who jettison plastic bags, the cars speeding down country roads, scattering koalas, wallabies and kangaroos. Summer should be reserved for the fauna and flora who better appreciate it. Summer is a time when she can visit Blue Lake on North Stradbroke Island to meditate and pay her respects to the long-departed dead of the Noonuccal tribe whose bodies were placed on rafts of paper bark, set alight and pushed into the centre of the spirit lake.

*T*he seasons bear personal memories and emotions for all Australians. In this reflection, four respected Australians and a host of photographers record their feelings.

Autumn

REG LIVERMORE

At the feet of gathering Winter
Autumn falls.
Lay down a Royal Flush of playing cards
as bright and burnished offerings of great selfless glory.
Cast-off coat of many colours,
our carpet and our bridge towards the coming dark.

WELL, ALL POETRY ASIDE, autumn's the time when the leaves drop. Some of us immediately tut and sigh, drag out our rakes, and set about turning our outdoors into spotless manifestations of domestic order, which seems to me a pointless exercise if the last leaf has not yet fallen. And why not enjoy the show? One of autumn's attractions, surely, is to pad across a stretch of ground which is thickly and softly carpeted with colours of an unforgettable sunset; and when the performance is over the wind usually obliges by clearing it away.

It doesn't always come in the same form, or at the same time; sometimes it's early and it comes and goes before the blink almost, and sometimes the leaves hang on with blood-red knuckles even into June when at last the chill winds conspire to disperse the reluctant stragglers. It is the one appointment on Nature's calendar I love above all others: a triumphant finale to the cycle which began in the spring months before, and a fitting tribute to the naked majesty of winter.

It is as if the ground has wrapped itself in glorious patchwork as the trees and shrubs put themselves to sleep in preparation for the seasons ahead. It is a sensational time, and those of us who are autumn watchers closely observe the telltale warnings of its approach. During the last weeks of summer there is always that moment when the air suddenly quickens quite markedly. One morning it takes us by surprise, and though it may not repeat itself for weeks, it signals the wind-down of those hot and heavy days, and proclaims what will virtually be a garden fashion parade.

For trees and shrubs it is a long haul from the first budding 'til the great shedding before winter, especially following summer which bleaches and exhausts their foliage to the limits of endurance. Mine also.

I can understand the majority preference for springtime and its range of bloom and blossom, but I can never quite see eye to eye with those who find autumn a time of great melancholy unless, of course, it is as I believe, that our own lives run a parallel of experience with the annual cycle in Nature. Some are actually quite depressed by it; for them perhaps the Fall is too much a final fling of glory before the winter of existence, the last hurrah before the demise. Well, for me the hope is that there will always be another spring, another round, the inevitability of day after night, and new energy after rest.

Apart from the conifers, firs and spruces, practically every tree in my garden is deciduous; indeed leaving apart the rhododendrons and azaleas, the shrubs are too. Purposely so that I am treated to major spectacles in all four seasons. After the privilege and intimacy of winter when everything stands bared, revealing the skeletal wonder of structure and shape, the young and delicate buds of spring burst into enthusiastic flower, turning quickly to the fecundity of summer when one can almost hear the growth, followed in turn by the culmination — autumn, whose colours are mature, stately and proud.

So I love my maples particularly because they are trees for all seasons. They have the ingenious and dazzling ability to bewitch the eyes at all times. Not to forget the birches! The beeches, the elms and the cherries, the nyssas, tulip trees and lindens. I love them all. And the shrubs do it too: to see *Fothergilla Major* in full flight, to mention but one of the treats, is spellbinding. I suppose the appreciation of one colour over another is a personal matter, so that I am quite simply captivated by the scarlets and reds, the yellows and gold, orange and russets, indeed the spectrum of burnished tones through to daring purple. And it's not that I don't gawp and wonder at the stylishness and sophistication of early spring because I do, but it does seem to deteriorate into a blowsy vulgarity as the season moves on so that the overall effect can be quite disconcerting. But autumn actually achieves dignity at its conclusion. How can the botanical experience not be likened to our earthly journey?

I guess the theatricality of it all is one of its greatest appeals for me. It is the grand transformation scene *par excellence*! It is Bakst and Benois, a design masterpiece. The landscape achieves a mantle of such intense vibrancy, colours which seem to glow in the now sharp air, and in the twilight especially there is always a breathtaking luminosity wrapped and caressed by fingers of smoke from early fires which curl and unfold from chimneys of every shape and size.

On the other hand I am not just a spectator in the garden: I live and work there, and my preferences may have much to do with degrees of effort and the requirements of time and attention demanded by specific seasons. So when autumn arives I am generally relieved of both anxiety and responsibility. I am able to shuffle about secure in the knowledge the lawn has ceased growing, that the weeds have mostly given up, and I know with winter ahead there is a stretch of time in which long promised chores can be addressed at leisure. Autumn walks through the garden are the lingering ones. There is time at last to think over the past and to contemplate the future. These thoughts can range wildly from the horticultural to the psychological, but in real terms it is taking stock. Wrapped in warm coats, pullover and scarves, the promenade beneath trees all hung with leaves like coloured party lanterns give one an overwhelming sense of a break-up celebration; that time before we go inside against the cold, light the fires and contemplate the toll and promise of our walk.

The sun sets on swamp
land outside Adelaide,
ahead of a cold night.

Pelicans dabble happily
in the chilly water on the
NSW coast near Eden.

Autumn leaves begin to
build their blanket . . .

. . . the blanket grows
thicker as the limbs grow
barer.

The first breath of
autumn taints the
poplars.

AUTUMN / 19

The golden vine leaves
hint at a golden crop.
RIGHT: The majestic
combination of green
and rust.

The last gasp of autumn;
a handful of leaves cling
grimly to their branches.

AUTUMN / 2 3

The Garden State,
Victoria, where the lakes
hold the tones of autumn
in their still mirrors.

Still life in autumn.

Whether you're walking
alongside the Torrens
Lake in Adelaide . . .

. . . or driving in the Blue
Mountains of NSW.
Autumn is distinctively
autumn.

ABOVE: In the lee of Mt
Beauty and nearby,
RIGHT: Lake Guy and
Bogong Village. Victorian
autumn splendour.

The stillness of a Victorian autumn. LEFT: Mists hover over the frail valley and RIGHT: The russet riverbank of Myrtleford.

Early morning mists are reluctant to leave the valley.

The tree-filled richness
of Bright, Victoria.

Bright from the
surrounding hilltops.

Gosh's Paddock in
Richmond, Vic . . . a
golden corner.

It could be an English
country lane not the
sunburnt country.

Leaves line the steps
leading to Burnham
Beeches, one of Victoria's
stateliest country resorts
and RIGHT: form a gentle
tablecloth on a riverbank
picnic slab.

The softness of Bright. The picturesque
Victorian town, on the fringe of Mt
Buffalo National Park is superb in
autumn.

Two ducks ignore the
chill autumn morning in
Canberra.

The clear still air
highlights the historic
remnants of Tasmania's
convict past at Port
Arthur.

Seppelts Winery in South
Australia.

The elegant gateway
leading to Melbourne's
Exhibition building.

Winter

BOB BROWN

When sleep shuts out
the winter's gale
with its freezing rain
and hail
that clatters on the iron,
then silence wakes me
to the still
the softest quiet,
I smile to myself
knowing
through the night
it's snowing.

WINTER IS THE freshener. It is the time for us to find ourselves and to think about the world. It is our hibernation from life's distractions. We do not, like so many of our fellow creatures, crawl into a hollow log to sleep. But there is a yearning for a fireside gathering of friends, toast from the burning embers and a mug of something warm, as the frosty air creeps in past the windowsill.

Winter is a clearing of the decks. It reminds us, above all, that nature is still in control and that the spin of planets, the tilting of Earth's axis to take us away from the Sun's fiercest glow, and the inscrutable mystery of existence in this wonderful Universe remain happily way beyond our control.

Even the greenhouse effect, showing how humanity's greatest impact on the Earth's environment is unwanted and through ignorance, rather that through the bliss of understanding, will come and go without the slightest threat to winter as an eternal part of life on Earth.

Years ago I went with friends into the Walls of Jerusalem in Tasmania's highlands. What a weekend. A mantle of soft snow was already over the land and the lakes were frozen. We talked of the thousand-foot-thick icecap which covered the region just 10,000 years ago. The ground was frozen solid beneath the snow and, overnight, the tent froze solid too. We woke with frost coating the inside and outside tent walls, and our boots like iron, the laces like heaving fencing wire. We needed a fire to thaw our socks which had set like slices of wood.

When we got going, I chased a wallaby through the snow and later stood in the centre of the beautiful Lake Salome where, just months before, we had swum in the warm waters of a heatwave. A kilometre away, my friends yelled 'hello!' from a hilltop, and the soundwaves' gentle pressure set a sound, like an express train, swishing across the ice, past me to the shore behind. The ice had cracked from end to end, down the middle of the pear-shaped lake and, to follow-up, a great cornice of snow then tumbled down from the crags of West Wall above us. There were countless gentle sighs in the silence as melting piles of snow were released from the branches of pencil pines by the morning sunshine.

I came back to camp exhilarated and exhausted. I felt like sitting and smiling, the sleeve of my will tugged at by the first fingers of hypothermia. I could well have stayed rather than face the three-hour trudge back down the mountain track to the cars.

My mind was alive with the thoughts of earlier years in the Great Dividing Range - a fox in the frosty moonlight; no water from the frosted pipes;

blackberry jam and cream on toast for breakfast; the crunch of ice from high-thrown stones landing on the New England farm pond; snow flurries swirling to Earth through the Eucalypts; the glide of skis down impossible, thrilling, glistening white slopes of the Snowy Mountains.

I love the winter. But never so much as in the last week of June 1982. Winter howled with rage across the western wilderness of Tasmania. Temperatures in the midland towns fell to a record minus 14 C, while snow closed highways throughout the island. A miraculous mantle of white covered even the ferny glades of the lower Franklin River near sea level where the last, hardy blockaders, from their camps hidden in the forest, kept vigil on the works at the Gordon-below-Franklin damsite. The freeze and blizzard stopped the bulldozers in their tracks. A quiet fell over the country, its wildness awaiting the death sentence if the High Court of Australia ruled in favour of the dam builders.

On July 1, midwinter's day, the High Court ruled, by four to three, to save the Franklin River. Winter's prescient halt to the destruction became a permanent reprieve for one of the world's most valuable natural valleys. Within days the bulldozers were being barged back out of the region.

In a country where folklore has it that the tropical heat blights our thinking, winter stirs old memories, quickens ideas for the future and often brings a warmth for each other which escapes the hurry of the rest of the year. Winter is for hugging.

Yet all of us have a limit to the chill. Whether camped in the great, starlit outback frost, or caught with a cold, or lost walking in the wretched wet of a rainsodden forest, winter can bring despair to its most ardent admirers. Yet, its miseries and moodiness are part of the challenge and diversity which makes the winter so special. And also makes it a time for being alone.

One winter morning, I got up before dawn. Frost in fantastic, crystalline patters had worked its way up the window panes. I had tea and toast by a quick, kindling fire, put on all my woollens, and headed for the Bluff. This lofty dolerite mountain rises to 1350 metres behind my house. As I moved through the forests the dawn was breaking. The birds began calling through the treetops. In the climbing gully the waterfall was almost fully frozen. Icicles, some a broom handle long, hung from the rocks. Sheaths of ice coursed down over the boulders.

Near the top, little trees and bushes were encased in ice, as if in solid multi-domed temples of glass. On the summit, snow covered the alpine herb fields and a mist rose to the first warming rays of the sun. A magnificient anthelion, the spangled arch of light thrown on the mist by the rising sun, gave colour in the almost total whiteness.

From the edge of the Bluff I looked down on the clusters of buildings marking each farm in the valley. Smoke was beginning to rise from the kitchen chimneys. The farms were still in the shadow, the paddocks were white with frost and the hilltops lit by the fising sun. It was like looking down on a hidden, miniature world.

I remember nothing of coming home. My mind is full of going there and being there. That's how winter is for me. I look forward to it, I relish being wrapped in it and care nothing for its passing.

It may not be florid, chic nor in great demand, but winter is the friendliest old coat in the cupboard.

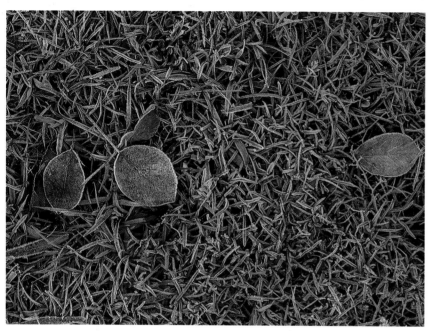

Frost, the sure sign of
winter's arrival, coats
suburban lawns and
country paddocks alike.

Winter's coats: TOP LEFT:
Eucalypts shiver in
Kosciusko National Park.
LEFT: Traces of snow linger
on a rockface sheltered
from the sun in the
Grampians, Vic. ABOVE:
The chilling slopes of
Mount Buller.

Even in mid-winter the distinctively
Australian sky shines clear and stark.
Victoria's Mount Hotham region
shimmers in this view from the top of
Brokhoff to Mount Feathertop.

Australia's High Country.
Modest by alpine
standards but just as cold!

Snow gums in the white
cover on Mount Buller.

LEFT: Snow gums stand boldly in the afternoon.
RIGHT: The morning sun has failed to melt the snow clinging to the branches.

LEFT: Morning mist on the
foothills of Mount Buller.
RIGHT: The stark beauty of
Tasmania's Cradle
Mountain.

WINTER / 67

LEFT: Sunset from the summit of Mount Buller. RIGHT: A pessimistic winter sky over Thredbo.

WINTER / 6 9

The Southern Alps. FROM LEFT: Cold grey, tepid gold, chilled white.

W I N T E R / 7 1

An icy eiderdown looking
across to Mt Stirling from
Buller.

Mt Hotham in Victoria: a
seasonal village.

The unlikely face of winter. In the tropical playground off the Queensland Coast winter means swimming, sunbathing, sailing.

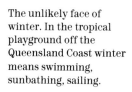

Spring shows the first
sign of yielding to winter
looking to snow-capped
Mount Buller

The forbidding waters of winter.

ABOVE: Jacksons Crossing
in East Gippsland and
RIGHT: A trout stream in
the Snowy Mountains.

Spring

ERIC ROLLS

AUSTRALIA MOVES by fits and starts. Our seasons do not acknowledge 1 September. Even changing hours of daylight influence exotic plants the most. Sow tomatoes for best yield when the hours are increasing, carrots when they are decreasing. Over much of Australia native plants must grow when it rains whatever the season. They might not get another opportunity for months.

When we lived at Boggabri we planted a weeping willow at the end of the kitchen drain. It grew quickly and we decided that each year its first leaf would mark the beginning of spring. All the family watched for it. One whole leaf had to present itself to earn the glad cry 'Spring is here!' because some years a bud would split and the tip of a leaf show, then the temperature would change and it dared not risk uncovering itself any more. The earliest it appeared was mid-July, the latest mid-October. At the same time — it was always after good rain — all plants sprang into sudden growth. In one week crops and pastures made a month's growth. It happens everywhere every year, some time between the cold weather and the hot. That is the spring. The word for the season has the same Germanic origin as spring meaning to jump. The lovely Chinese character for spring shows a plant coming to life after the

thaw. A seedling warmed by the sun, ⊖ , twists its stem, ⌐ , as it tries to push through the hard ground, ▬ .
Once it breaks the surface the cotyledons open, ⨯⨯⨯ .
These symbols all combine in the one old pictogram for chun, spring, 曽 .
Over the centuries scholars and artists refined it into a character that would exhibit their brush strokes, and their sense of balance.

After the regular visitation of winter snow over so much of China, spring is such a definite season it divides into six joints and breaths of a fortnight each, the Beginning of spring, Spring Rains, the Feast of Excited Insects, the Vernal Equinox, Clear and Bright, Grain Rain.

The grain rain must come much earlier in Australia. Except in the southern districts it is usually not summer's job to ripen crops sown at the end of autumn or the beginning of winter. The principal rain must follow soon after the spring burst since there are so many more leaves to feed. Once it comes, flagged shoots lift up out of the wheat plants. One can draw them out easily and slide finger and thumb down their sappy lengths to feel the little bulges of the heads. They might be no more than 15 mm long but one can see where the grains will form. The noded grain stem pushes the growing head through a cylinder. In our district it lifts clear of the flag in mid-spring, it flowers, it fills. The farmer's year's work is in flower, his lifetime of knowledge modified kindly or savagely by the weather. A freak late frost can destroy a crop, so can a week of blazing heat when it is in flower but good rains until the grain is doughy, a drying-off to harden it, then hot weather for harvest can build it into magnificence: work, knowledge and plant yielding their utmost. The testing of the first grain is a farmer's late spring joy. Snap off a golden head — the stem is now brittle. Grind it in the cupped left palm with the heel of the right hand. Blow away awn and husk, grind a little more, blow again, There might be 60 grains, flint hard and almost translucent. Chew them. In a minute or so a ball of gluten forms in the mouth. It is a wonder to put the header into such a crop. It brings more than profit: the soil has justified one.

In the Top End, that wondrous part of Australia so many Australians never see, there are no conventional seasons, there is a Wet and a Dry. The changeover begins some time after mid-October with a lift in humidity. The Baobab trees respond. One week their huge bulbous trunks support apparently dead branches, the next week masses of big white flowers. No leaves interfere with the display. It is a passion of flowers only. At the same time the termite mounds, one to three metres high, seem to break into flower. New red bulges protrude out of weathered grey pillars. Thousands of workers are making room for those that will hatch to feed on new grass when the rains come.

Lake Eyre has a spring once or twice a century when rivers and creeks of dry sand flow water for a change and pour it metres deep into its huge salt pans. Swans, pelicans, herons, gulls, fish, frogs breed there in hundreds of thousands. For a couple of years the lake is livelier than it was when it was an ancient sea. Then it dries up. Fish and frogs die in stinking masses, the fittest of the birds fly out to establish themselves somewhere else as superior representatives of their species. They have to survive a dry flight of hundreds of kilometres. I have seen three young Lake Eyre pelicans resting on one of our smaller farm ground tanks before carrying on to the coast. They looked like yachts in a backyard swimming pool. It was probably their first stop in 1,200 km.

The rains that spring the grasses in the Tanami Desert come in sudden storms. Black clouds build above the reds and blues and mauves of the flats and ridges, then they break up into individual storms, perhaps a dozen, that scatter across the desert in narrow paths. Two storms might race one another a hundred metres apart with the sun streaming down between them. Creeks run for an hour or so and empty nowhere, but all along them insects hatch, or break out of chrysalises, especially moths in thousands. They have no time to feed. They mate, lay eggs, and die. As adults their spring is the whole of life and it lasts a few hours of one night. Most of them have not even been given a name. They have no place in the population of the world.

As I write this a silt trap on our biggest farm dam is busy with animals. A white-faced heron patrols its edges in turn with a white-necked heron. Yabbies shoot backwards from the shallows. Tadpoles and water beetles break the surface. Dragonflies and their associates whirr overhead in mating loops, then the females pull their tails free and the males circle low over the water still grasping the females behind the head with their anal claspers and dip down every now and then so that she can trail her ovipositor in the water and lay her eggs. Only three days ago this tank had been dry for months. We had a good storm late in the evening, it filled, and by early morning yabbies had come up from watery pockets two or three metres underground, so had frogs. They had mated already and the females had laid their eggs. The black-specked froth floated in clumps. The urgency of life in Australia constantly amazes me. Apparently sterile dust becomes a busy pool of water in a few hours. The great Murray River once knew spring excitement every year. Before the dams on its upper waters were built, snow thawing on the ranges in New South Wales and Victoria began to lift its water level about September. A few hot days, a good rain sent floodwaters down, and a succession of ducks responded. Grey teal reacted first. As soon as the banks overflowed into lagoons, flocks of male and female began patrolling them. They flew high from one lagoon to the next, they wheeled, skimmed the water, turned again. If the water kept on rising, the males formed separate flocks and began courtship displays. They splashed down into the water, trod it and thrashed their wings, bounced across it, swam in circles, lifted into the air and splashed down again. For several days the females took little notice of them. They wisely watched the water level. If it rose high enough, they selected one of the posturing males, mated and looked for a nesting site. Their young feed on plants as well as water creatures. Black ducks waited a week or so longer for animal life to build up in the water. Hardheads nested when the waters reached out to the lignum and cumbungi swamps, then they had the deep water they prefer to feed in to fall back on. The beautiful pink-eared ducks with spectacular zebra stripes on neck and flanks bred after the water began to drop in the lagoons. Then the water was warm enough to produce blooms of plankton for their ducklings. Yellowbelly and silver perch, washed out into the lagoons, also spawned as the water temperature rose. In the next flood adults and fingerlings washed back into the river. Now the Murray is little more than an irrigation channel. It has lost all the seasons.

Of native plants, acacias most appreciate spring. They celebrate it more or less according to the weather. I wrote a short poem about the wondrous spring of 1974 in the Pilliga Forest that forms our northern boundary.

> *September comes in always yellow and raw umber.*
> *In the scrub acacias are in bloom in hundred acre patches.*
> *It is trite to write of spring and wattle blossom*
> *So just let me record this:*
> *I live where miracles are commonplace.*

That spring some species of acacia bloomed in 400 ha masses. Branches trailed on the ground with the weight of blossom, they met overhead across the tracks and dropped flowers three centimetres deep. One drove through yellow tunnels. There were white wattles, cream, all the ranges of yellow in spikes and balls. The buttery yellow of cassia overlay it in patches. Purple false sarsaparilla climbed stumps and shrubs. Angophora and bloodwood stood white with flowers. White cypress pine spurted pollen in heavy brown clouds. Red, blue, mauve, white shrubs of fifty species displayed in masses. Rosy pink drosera carpeted the ground on the Broom plains. Hundreds of thousands of hectares of marvellous garden began at our back gate.

And if we had been away on research, even if I had been writing a different book then, I might have missed it. It lasted a fortnight at its best. Now conditions have changed. Trees have grown and occluded the understorey. There might never be another spring like it. In Australia one must keep constantly aware. So much that is marvellous happens once in a lifetime.

Melbourne, the garden city, reflects
the serenity of spring. And Western
Australia's 'Everlasting' wildflowers
revel in the spring sunshine.

The vivacious coastal
daisy (*Olearia rudis*) near
Augusta.

LEFT: Surprising Canberra. Blossoms frame the Captain Cook water jet (top) and the Telecom Tower. ABOVE: Mount Isa, the bustling and burly mining town with a soft heart.

SPRING / 93

ABOVE and RIGHT: Roadside
displays in Western
Australia, the wildflower
state.

Salvation Jane or
Patterson's Curse which
runs rampant in the
Flinders Ranges region.

LEFT: West Australian wildflowers in a natural display. ABOVE: Petunias, a spring favourite.

ABOVE AND RIGHT: The red
bottlebrush (Callistemon
spp)

ABOVE: A spectacular Austral grass tree in the Flinders Range and RIGHT: A slash of red brightens in Western Australia's Sterling Ranges.

The Sturt Desert Pea,
native to dry outback
regions and floral
emblem of South
Australia.

LEFT: Fragile spring colour. ABOVE: The Mangles' Kangaroo Paw, floral emblem of West Australia.

Wildflowers of Western
Australia . . .

. . . a never-ending
panorama

LEFT: Common Billy's Buttons (*Craspedia uniflora*) found along the coast and tablelands in all states. ABOVE: The Poached Egg Daisy (*Myriocephalus stuartii*).

Floral displays at
Melbourne.

TOP: A Brisbane spring garden. ABOVE: Spring display in the Royal Tasmanian Botanical Gardens.

Peppers Resort in the
Hunter Valley (top) and
the Dandenong Ranges
of Victoria.

Northern Tasmania, an
idyllic rural season.

LEFT: The gently rolling pastures of Wynyard on the North Coast of Tasmania. ABOVE: The blunter features of South Australia's Flinders Ranges.

An unhurried muster
near Boonoke, NSW.

LEFT: Daffodils, the
traditional face of spring.
ABOVE: *Linara*, better
known as toad flax.

Wildflowers at their best
and most varied in
Western Australia.

The wattle, Australia's
national floral emblem

Acacia suaveolens, a common wattle around Sydney.

Summer

O O D G E R O O
O F T H E T R I B E N O O N U C C A L
(FORMERLY KATH WALKER)

LIVING ON MINJERRIBAH (Stradbroke Island) is beautiful all year round. Minjerribah is situated about sixteen kilometres from mainland Australia, off the coast of Cleveland, Queensland and is the grass-root home of the Noonuccal tribe.

I welcome summer's yearly appearance here. To awaken to the dawn of another day, listening to the happy twitter of baby birds in their nest. The first call of the kookaburra at five o'clock in the morning and then again at six o'clock is better than any man-made awakener. Truly they have earned the title of 'The Bushman's Alarm Clock'.

The early call of the kookaburras and their young, trying to copy their call is a delight to hear. Young kookaburra chicks have to learn to laugh, they are not born laughers. I have discovered that like all children, some are fast learners, some average and some slow.

Before dawn breaks, the storm bird is calling to his mate. After mating they seek out a nest for the female to lay her eggs. Usually, the fryer birds are the victims. After hatching the storm birds' chicks, the fryers become very angry and do their best to throw the baby storm birds out of their nest. This pattern is repeated every summer.

By 9.00 a.m. the bush is alive with the call of the cicadas and the melodious voice of the thrush can be heard as she and her mate flit from branch to branch, eating their breakfast of golden orb spiders.

There is a rustle of dry leaves and I know old man goanna is sneaking through the undergrowth in search of a victim.

A carpet snake stealthily climbs the high pine trees in search of birds' eggs. The battle for reproduction ensues as crows join together to peck him off his perch and away from their eggs. Their cries of anguish echo and re-echo through the tall pines.

All creatures welcome the electrical storms, for they energise and strengthen the land and all her creatures.

To walk the low tide in search of oysters and quampies (pearl shell) is an experience rewarded by the feast when they are cooked on the open fire.

Going to the outside beach, where the Pacific Ocean washes daily the thirty-seven kilometres of white sandy beach. Doing the eugarie (pippi) twist in search of the fat shell fish, lying just beneath the rolling, shore bound waves.

Fishing from my flat-bottom, three-metre aluminium dinghy, for summer whiting and bream, around the mangrove trees. Rowing over to check the dilly pots for blue claw sand crabs. Taking my dogs for their daily swim in the placid waters of the great sea spirit, Quandamooka (Moreton Bay). Watching their efforts at trying to catch fish.

Marvelling at Nature's way of working with the moon to bring us the high two and three metre tides.

The gathering of seaweed for my garden, washed up on the beach after a strong westerly blow.

Going swimming in the warm waters of Brown Lake, three kilometres inland.

Watching the beautiful colours of the sunset, as the sun disappears over the western horizon.

When night appears to swallow the last of the daylight, I hear the heavy growl of old man koala claiming his territorial rights. His mate is busy teaching their young ones how to climb from limb to limb, from tree to tree.

Revisiting Myora Springs as it empties its tumbling waters into the bay.

Lighting a small smoke fire to keep the mosquitoes and sandflies away.

Catching my breath at the beauty of the cork tree in flower. Their long branches of deep green leaves, contrasting with their clusters of mauve flowers.

Hearing the fruit bats quarrelling in the tall gum trees as they suck the honey from the gum's cream-puff flowers.

The book-book owl calling his mournful call of the 'book-book - book-book'. He is our message bringer. He also protects us from the white spirit owl of death.

The sea curlew calling from the mud flats at low tide.

The summer rain beating out a tune in monotonous repetition during the big wet. The dry sandy soil, welcoming its cool contact.

The pine trees losing the last of their smoky blooms, as a bird lands on their green leaves, shaking the heavy pollen into the air, which to the naked eye looks like the pines are on fire.

The deep, almost indigo, blue colour of a cloudless sky. Night brings stars into focus and I marvel at the bear, the evening star, the saucepan, the Milky Way and I remember the Aboriginal legend of the seven sisters.

When the moon has grown to full size, watching the nocturnal animals and night birds going about their nightly business.

Comes morning and a willy wagtail chatters and darts about catching the flying insects coming from the smoky pines. The bronze winged pigeons strut about, puffing out their chests, looking for seeds on the ground.

All these happenings do not happen every day or night. It comes after many years of my watching and learning from the Earth Mother and her beautiful creations. I spend my spare time, listening and learning about her beautiful balance of all living things.

I am sad when I see the cane toad hopping all over the land, having been bought to the island under the bonnets of the four wheel drive cars. The tourists, who in many cases, act like terrorists, dropping their rubbish over the land and bespoiling the beaches.

My anger at their fear on seeing a snake and killing it. Their mad rush across the island bringing death to kangaroos, wallabies, koalas and bird life. Their young people stealing mainland cars and abandoning them in out of way bush tracks. Their irresponsible habit of partying on the high cliffs at the far end of Minjerribah, at Point Lookout. Sometimes, ending in tragedy for some of them as they fall to their deaths from the high cliffs.

Watching the dolphins riding the waves from those same cliffs, swimming with the surf riders, quietens my anger and leaves me with another type of sadness, a kind of uneasy peace. I wonder whether all the human race will ever learn to live in peace and harmony with the Earth Mother and her sea spirits.

I visit Blue Lake, the spirit lake of the Noonuccal tribe, to meditate, to pay my respects to our long departed dead, whose bodies were placed on rafts of paper bark, set fire to and pushed out into the middle of the lake, so they could sleep their last deep sleep in the arms of the water spirit of the lake's deep waters.

I visit the last of our remaining middens, piled high with the long ago discarded shells and bones, now overgrown with shrubs and ferns. My anger rises again as I notice the roads made by the miners which cut deep into the middens. I have been told, this is not desecration, that this particular exercise is called progress.

I watch the lifesavers at Point Lookout guarding the summer visitors from harm. Feeling deep sorrow when they risk their lives to bring back to shore a lifeless body that was once a happy laughing human being. Summer brings with it the laughter, the tragedy.

The heat of the summer morning air disappears with the arrival of the cool afternoon sea breezes blowing themselves from across the bay.

The ti-trees' heavily scented blooms become decorated with the beautifully coloured lorrikeets, screeching their happiness and well-being from the swamp lands.

Last summer I saw a sad pelican riding the waves close to shore on the outside beach. He was guarding his dead mate being washed back and forth by the rolling surf of the incoming tide. I wondered how she had met her death. Was a speeding car racing along the beach responsible? I really couldn't tell. A great sadness overtook me and I walked away wishing I had the ability to stop some of the sad things that happen during our summers. I found a huge pile of eugaries (pippi) above high water mark, their shells opened and gasping for sea water, I take them back to the surf knowing most of them will die: knowing too, some thoughtless human being had dumped them in their hurry to get home. I rationalise, they won't die in vain. The seagulls and eugarie birds will appreciate the unexpected feast.

Watching the sunrise from the outside beach always brings an overwhelming calmness within me. The ball rises out of the horizon and records its reflection in the Pacific Ocean.

Overseas liners stand out against the sky line, making their way to the port of Brisbane. I note the rubbish that has been dumped overboard, coming slowly in on the incoming tide, pieces of plastic, bottles and tin cans decorate the white sands. I found a discarded syringe once, lying in a tuft of grass, I swept it up with a piece of plastic and dumped it in the industrial bin.

On the bay side of the island, the beautiful sea eagles have built a huge nest high up on a large gum tree. They sit on the mangrove trees proud and free, watching for fish movements in the tide. I count twenty pelicans cruising along outside the mangroves.

When I take my fishing gear to the beach they come paddling in closer waiting for me to clean my catch and throw the gut into the water. As I move back to the land, they come squabbling in competing with each other for the gutted remains.

The summers of Minjerribah are movements of actions and all living things are our reminders of the Earth Mother's balancing of her realm.

Only man, through his greed disrupts, destroys, maims and kills her balance. How many more summers will Minjerribah have to endure before man learns to live in peace and harmony with her elements? When will he ever learn that Earth was created for all living things?

The rocks of the island are her sentries. They are mute reminders that they are her temples, that we have inherited from our Rainbow Serpent, our Earth Mother.

We, her children, know it is our duty to take care of her creations and pass them on when our time comes to return to the loving arms of our Earth Mother.

Therefore, we know too, we cannot own the land — the land owns us. All seasons are precious gifts to all living things to be shared with all.

The summer moon casts
its clear light.

Moreton Island,
Queensland . . . where
the sun *really* shines.

Twilight and evening
warmth . . . ideal for rock
fishing and sailing.

A sultry summer storm
broods over Ayers Rock.

Bicentennial celebrations
on Sydney Harbour.

A sudden summer storm
sweeps up in outback NSW.

Summer in the Northern Territory means the Big Wet. LEFT: Barramundi Gorge and RIGHT: Fogg Dam near Darwin.

Sugar cane burning in
Queensland.

Wheat harvesting in
Victoria

TOP: Lifesavers in Australia start young . . . girls or boys. And paddle furiously!

On the beach at
Surfers Paradise

Kooyong, for many
years the home of the
Australian Open.

Windsurfing in the
choppy sea off the
Northern Beaches of
Sydney . . .

. . . or in the calm of a
basin marina. It's a
summer delight.

Summer sunsets and the
water . . . an Australian
combination that creates
a peace all its own.

The sun feels good. For families . . .
. . . and for lovers on Kangaroo Island, SA.

Rows of lavender create
purple arcs over a hill on
a lavender farm in
Nabowla, Tas.

Summer fun. ABOVE: Just another day in the tropics. FACING PAGE. TOP LEFT: Beach netball, portable and instant. TOP RIGHT: Bowls, a traditional recreation with a huge following. BOTTOM: The water slide at Queensland's Dreamworld.

A spectacular aerial view
of Rottnest Island, the
playground in the West.

The Sydney-Hobart yacht
race, with the small boats
underfoot as usual in the
annual summer racing
classic.

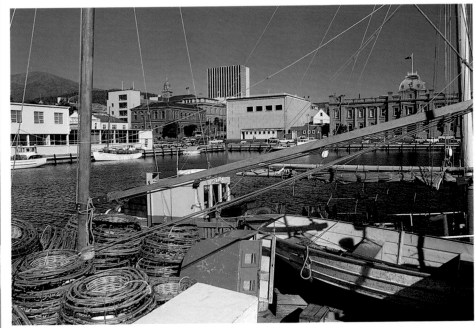

Summer in the south . . .
LEFT: Maslins Beach,
deserted and moody.
ABOVE: Hobart, peaceful
and historic.

Summer rain has
swamped Lake Menindee
in the Kinchega National
Park, 100km south-west
of Broken Hill.

Summer about to fade to autumn on the banks of Melbourne's Yarra River.

The endless summer,
Australian style.

Summer in the outback.
Gums, blue sky, and
burnt rocks.

Sand dunes in Discovery
Bay National Park,
Victoria.

Two faces of summer: the Twelve
Apostles in Port Campbell National
Park, moody in the setting sun. And
the Gold Coast, home to sun-seekers.

Credits:

P2. Otto Rogge, Stock Photos
P4. Otto Rogge, Stock Photos
P6. John Carnemolla, Stock Photos
P14. Australian Tourist Commission
P15. Australian Tourist Commission
P16. Rick Altman, Stock Photos
P17. Rick Altman, Stock Photos
P18. Otto Rogge, Stock Photos
P20. Australian Tourist Commission
P21. Australian Tourist Commission
P23. Otto Rogge, Stock Photos
P24. Liana Frances, Stock Photos
P25. Upper: Ian Lawrence, Stock Photos Lower: Pavi Steel, Stock Photos
P26. Gabby Lowen, Stock Photos
P27. Left: Paul Steel, Stock Photos. Right: Gabe Palmer, Stock Photos
P28. Australian Tourist Commission
P29. Tony Martorano, Stock Photos
P30. Stock Photos
P31. Paul Steel, Stock Photos
P32. Jean Pierre Grech, Stock Photos
P33. Gary Lewis, Stock Photos
P34. Otto Rogge, Stock Photos
P36. James B. Walshe, AusChromes
P37. Ken Stepnell, Stock Photos
P38. Kelvin Aitken, AusChromes
P39. Owen Hughes, AusChromes
P40. Australian Tourist Commission
P41. Otto Rogge, Stock Photos
P42. Otto Rogge, Stock Photos
P44. Australian Tourist Commission
P45. Australian Tourist Commission
P46. Australian Tourist Commission

P47. Tony Martorano, Stock Photos
P53. Australian Tourist Commission
P54. Bill Bachman, Stock Photos
P55. Otto Rogge, Stock Photos
P56. Upper: Bill Bachman, Stock Photos. Lower: Australian Tourist Commission.
P57. Bill Bachman, Stock Photos.
P58. Bill Bachman, Stock Photos
P60. Bill Bachman, Stock Photos
P62. Bill Bachman, Stock Photos
P64. Australian Tourist Commission
P65. Bill Bachman, Stock Photos
P66. Bill Bachman, Stock Photos
P67. Owen Hughes, AusChromes
P68. Bill Bachman, Stock Photos
P69. Bill Bachman, Stock Photos
P70. Bill Bachman, Stock Photos
P71. Otto Rogge, Stock Photos
P72. Bill Bachman, Stock Photos
P74. Bill Bachman, Stock Photos
P76. Upper: Stuart Owen Fox. Lower: Australia Tourist Commission
P77. Bill Bachman, Stock Photos
P78. Bill Bachman, Stock Photos
P79. Terry Murray, Stock Photos
P80. James B. Walshe, AusChromes
P81. Australian Tourist Commission
P88. Australian Tourist Commission
P89. Australian Tourist Commission

P90. Australian Tourist Commission
P91. Australian Tourist Commission
P92. Australian Tourist Commission
P93. Australian Tourist Commission
P94. Australian Tourist Commission
P95. Australian Tourist Commission
P96. Australian Tourist Commission
P97. Australian Tourist Commission
P98. Margaret Walton, AusChromes
P99. Australian Tourist Commission
P100. Australian Tourist Commission
P101. Bruno Jean Grasswill
P102. Australian Tourist Commission
P103. Bruno Jean Grasswill
P105. Australian Tourist Commission
P106. Australian Tourist Commission
P107. Australian Tourist Commission
P108. Australian Tourist Commission
P109. Australian Tourist Commission
P110. Australian Tourist Commission
P111. Australian Tourist Commission
P112. Australian Tourist Commission
P113. Upper: Stuart Owen Fox. Lower: Australian Tourist Commission.
P114. Upper: Australian Tourist Commission. Lower: Margaret Walton, AusChromes
P115. Australian Tourist Commission
P116. Peter Walton, AusChromes
P117. Jean Pierre Grech, Stock Photos.

P118. Australian Tourist Commission
P119. Australian Tourist Commission
P120. Australian Tourist Commission
P121. Bruno Jean Grasswill
P122. Peter Walton, AusChromes
P123. Australian Tourist Commission
P124. Australian Tourist Commission
P125. Australian Tourist Commission
P132. Otto Rogge, Stock Photos
P134. Australian Tourist Commission
P136. Australian Tourist Commission
P137. Australian Tourist Commission
P139. Australian Tourist Commission
P140. Australian Tourist Commission
P142. Australian Tourist Commission
P144. Australian Tourist Commission
P145. Australian Tourist Commission
P146. Australian Tourist Commission
P147. Australian Tourist Commission
P148. Australian Tourist Commission
P149. Australian Tourist Commission
P150. Australian Tourist Commission
P152. Australian Tourist Commission
P153. Australian Tourist Commission
P154. Bruno Jean Grasswill
P155. Australian Tourist Commission
P156. Australian Tourist Commission
P157. Australian Tourist Commission
P158. Margaret Walton, AusChromes

P160. Australian Tourist Commission
P161. Upper left: Australian Tourist Commission. Upper right: Stuart Owen Fox. Lower: Australian Tourist Commission.
P162. Australian Tourist Commission
P163. Australian Tourist Commission
P164. Australian Tourist Commission
P165. Australian Tourist Commission
P166. Otto Rogge, Stock Photos
P168. Otto Rogge, Stock Photos
P170. Otto Rogge, Stock Photos
P172. Otto Rogge, Stock Photos
P173. Peter Walton, AusChromes
P174. Australian tourism Commission
P175. Ken Stepnell, Stock Photos